THE CHRISTMAS PROMISE

WRITTEN BY:

Alison Mitchell

ILLUSTRATED BY:

Catalina Echeverri

A long, long time ago — so long that it's hard to imagine — God promised a new King.

He wasn't any ordinary King, like the ones we see on tv or in books. He would be different.

He would be a **NEW KING;**

a **RESCUING KING;**

a **FOREVER KING!**

And do you Know what? One precious night God Kept his Christmas promise. Would you like to Know how he did it?

The Christmas story starts with an angel.
WHOOSH! He came from God to see Mary.

The angel had a special message.

"Mary, you're going to have a baby.
   He will be a special baby. God promises
that your baby is going to be King
– not for a little time, but for ever and ever.
He will be the **FOREVER KING!**"

Mary was going to marry Joseph,
so God sent another angel.
WHOOSH! He came to see Joseph.
The angel had a special message.

"Mary is going to have a very special baby," the angel said to Joseph.

"Her baby is going to be King, and will rescue his people. He will be a RESCUING KING!"

God had promised that his new King would
be born in a little city called Bethlehem.
And that's where Mary and Joseph went.

But Bethlehem was very busy with lots and **lots** and **LOTS** of people.

So when the baby was born,
he had to sleep in a manger
instead of a bed.

All the other mangers in Bethlehem held food
for hungry animals to munch.
But this manger held a tiny baby.

He was God's special NEW KING!

The shepherds in the fields had such a surprise.
It was quiet and dark, and the sheep were snoozing,
when WHOOSH! – an angel popped into the sky!
Now the sky was bright, and the shepherds were
so, so scared,
But the angel had a special message for them...

"DON'T BE AFRAID! I have wonderful good news for you!" the angel said. "God's chosen King has been born tonight. He is going to rescue his people, just as God promised. He will be the RESCUING KING!" Then lots and lots of other excited angels joined in to celebrate.

The shepherds were really excited!
They went rushing to see the new King.
And there he was – lying in a manger
– just as the angel said.

But they weren't the only ones who had heard
the good news about the promised new King...

Some wise men living far, far away had also been sent a message.

It was quiet and dark, and they were watching the stars, when WHOOSH! – a new star popped into the sky!

The star had a special message.
The wise men knew what it meant...

A very special King had been born —
the King for all God's people.
This child was the promised NEW KING!

The wise men were so excited! So they went on a LOOOONG journey to see the new King.

And there he was – just as the star had shown them.

Everything God promised came true.

There are lots and lots of different Kings in the world, but God sent the greatest King of all! He sent:

a NEW KING;
a RESCUING KING;
a FOREVER KING.

And do you know what this King's name is?

His name is...

JESUS!

HOW DO WE KNOW
ABOUT THE CHRISTMAS PROMISE?

The main events of the first Christmas were written down for us by Matthew and Luke in the New Testament part of the Bible.

You will find them in Matthew 1 v 18-21 & 2 v 1-12, and in Luke 1 v 26-33 & 2 v 1-20.

But God started making promises about his new King thousands of years before Jesus was born. You will find some of these promises in the Old Testament.

They include:

Someone who will bring good to all people
(Genesis 12 v 1-3, 22 v 18, 28 v 14)

Someone who will be King for ever
(2 Samuel 7 v 11b-13; Daniel 7 v 13-14)

Someone who will save all kinds of people
(Isaiah 53 v 4-6)

Books and resources available in
"The Christmas Promise" series:

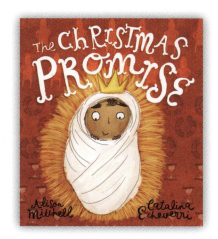

Storybook

Activity Book

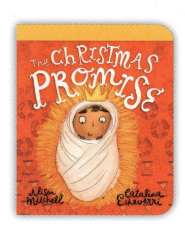

Board Book

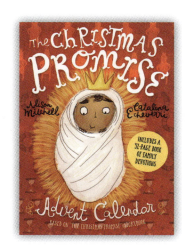

Advent Calendar

TALES that Tell the TRUTH

Enjoy all of the award-winning
"Tales That Tell The Truth" series:

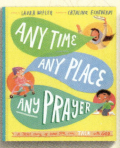  

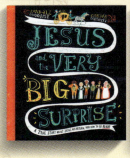